# Fool's Gold



Kelly Brady

BookLeaf Publishing

Presentation by *BookLeaf Publishing*

Web: www.bookleafpub.com

E-mail: info@bookleafpub.com

ISBN: 9789357212342

First edition 2023

# DEDICATION

This book is dedicated to my son, D.

Thank you for always laughing with me.

# Remember

Today brings new beginnings.
It is letting go of the past, the hurt and the trauma.
It is about living my authentic self and being true to me.
Sharing my love with those who are deserving and those who value me.
No more self doubt. I am loved. I am valued. I am worthy.
No more judgement. I have permission to live my life the way I want to.
No more holding back. I have the courage to fulfill my dreams without being held back by fear of being judged.
It doesn't matter what others believe, only what is right to me, and for me.
Remember by north. Remember by south.
Remember my east. Remember my west.
Remember my ancestors and their love and support.
Remember their eyes and hearts full of love, wanting the best for me.
My authentic self. Manifest what I want and remember this.
Remember what my heart wants. Manifest my desires.

Remember who I am and what my strengths are.
Remember the things that are holding me back.
Remember my ego is irrelevant, it is not my core being.
Remember happiness comes from within
Remember my ability to get back up when I am down.
Today brings new beginnings.
Make the most of it, I may not have a tomorrow.

# Don't Say You're Sorry

You say you are sorry.
So very sorry.
But I know the truth.
You are not sorry for me.
You are sorry for you.
Sorry that loneliness has crept in
and is now crushing you.
Don't say you are sorry.
When I know the truth.

# Gin Daze

Laughter, games, family and fun
Flowers, sand, birds and sun
Food, books, beach and shells
Crystals, love, dogs and bluebells
Sunsets, sunrises, sand and waves
All surrounding me in a gin daze

# Offspring

I may be annoying but at least I am colourful.
I am not smiling today; I did enough of that yesterday.
Are they my socks you are about to wear?
Cornflakes make me poo.
I forgot it was Christmas and I wanted to sleep in.
A jellyfish hugged me today.
If you pick me up early, I think I will like you.
My favourite place to go is to stay at home.

# Blue Heaven

The wind whispers to me
over the turmoil of the waves
"Feel the coolness of the breeze on your face.
Open your mouth so it is the salt air you taste.
Gaze to the horizon and look across the sea"
I listen to the wind knowing that Blue Heaven is
waiting for me.

# Stillness

Water ripples across the surface,
Erupting from the movement underneath.
The same as my thoughts and emotions,
Simmering through my inner being and out of
my skin.
Goosebumps. Smile. Tears.
Remember to breathe.
Breathe. Breathe.
Bring the stillness to me,
Watch the water ripples disappear.

# Road Trip

The car is packed, we are ready to go
Road tripping today, family tomorrow
Belting out tunes, us singing along
It always seems to be to our favourite song
Pointing out landmarks and nature along the way
22 'are we there yets', not yet I say
I'm hungry, Mum and I need the toilet too
Multiple stops, we'll get there soon
I'm hungry again, what is to eat?
Mum, can I please have another treat?
I ate the last one, there are none left I'm sorry,
But there is plenty of fruit, don't you worry!
Hunger soon forgotten, we see the sign
We have finally made it and right on time!
A feeling of relief washes over me,
We have made it; we are finally here!

# A Room with a City View

The sun creeps into my room
I can feel it on my face
Peeling back my eyelids
Rising from a sleepy daze
I step towards the window
And look out to the sky
Grateful for this day
In a room nine stories high
The room may be silent but
The hustle starts down below
I take a deep breath and salute the sun's glow
So far from home and the southern sea air
Watching the people below rush by without a
care
In my mind's eye I picture the ocean blue
But for now, I'm stuck in a room with a city
view

# Rain Tears

Rain drops race down the window
Like tears streaming down my face
Reminding me of what could have been
But now that is long gone
It eats me up, it feels so wrong
Time to let it all go
Let it all out and start again tomorrow

# Plastic World

The irony is we live in a plastic world where
almost everything breaks us down,
yet to rebuild ourselves we want the work to be
done by a 3D printer.

# Out

Sometimes we let the wrong people in
Then we don't know how to let them back out
Lust, passion, addiction and sin
I wonder what was that all about
Then our paths cross again
It makes me want to scream and shout
I want you back in
But you must stay out.

Stay away.
Far, far away.
There is no doubt.
You are out.

# Drowning in the Darkness

Is it so easy to fall into the abyss of your own thoughts without noticing how deep you have fallen until you are drowning in the darkness.

# The Man

Why must this man stand so close?
Why does this man like the sound of his own voice?
He steps forward. I step away
Can't he see he's invading my space?
My body language tells him
He just stares at me and grins
I think 'Get out of my way'
Yet it is 'Excuse me', I say
Polite I must be to this man
Because of who he is and where I am
I try to pass but we dance
The man with an air of arrogance

# Shower Thoughts

Shampoo doesn't sound like something you
would want to put on your head.
My singing is no better in the shower.
I wonder what gherkins dipped in hummus
would taste like.
Society has forgotten virtues like patience,
humility and compassion.
Why is it called the world wide web when there
are still places on earth that don't have the
internet?
No one will love me as much as I love myself.
Sometimes the wind sounds like it is sharing
nature's secrets.
Some people should come with a warning sign.
Why do we pretend spoons are planes when we
feed babies and toddlers, then tell them they
shouldn't play with their food as they get older?
Some people are evil covered in fat.
I should have had a bath.

# Fool's Gold

He promised her the world
She took it with both hands
She didn't know external forces
Had other plans
The love she had for him
Burned her soul
The illusion soon crashed down
Nothing left but devastation
Thoughts tightly wrapped
Deep seeded memories trapped
Detachment and avoidance
Moving on with reluctance
Thought we would grow old
Nothing but Fool's Gold

# Darkness

When darkness surrounds you, face it front on and swallow it whole.

# Permission

I have permission to respond with silence.
Silence is as clear as any words said out loud.
I have permission to say no.
No is an acceptable answer to anything I don't want to do.
I have permission to leave whenever I want to.
I don't have to provide an explanation.
I have permission to do things for myself and on my own.
Self care is important for my mental health.
I have permission to be my authentic self.
Judgement is a reflection of others.

# A Boy Named D

There once was a boy named D
Who was funny but liked to disagree
His Mum would go mad
And D would get sad
And she'd say, "Why don't you listen to me?"

There once was a boy named D
Giggling out loud with glee
Running naked through the house
Scurrying around like a mouse
Shouting, "You can't see me!"

There once was a boy named D
Who was funny as he could be
Vivacious, clever and caring
Kind, loving and daring
D is the best thing to happen to me

# Alternate Universe

Fresh spring water
Nature will provide
No outside influence
Crisp sea air
Abundance of nature
Hunt and gather
Takes a village
Sustainable lifestyle
Natural surroundings
Share and barter
The simple life

# Being Single

Being single does not equal loneliness.
Being single does not equal unhappiness.
Being single does not equal neediness.
Being single does not equal unworthiness.
Being single equals not settling.
Being single equals independence.
Being single equals freedom.
Being single equals self love.

# Words of Wisdom

Great wisdom is only achieved through great mistakes.
Don't spend too long looking back, you might step over an opportunity.
If you need something done, ask a busy person.
Always show kindness to animals.
Start your day with what you are grateful for.
Life is too short to clean skirting boards - go to the beach.
Remember your shopping bags when you go to the supermarket.
Walk as much as you can.
Scroll less and use your time more productively.
Listen to your favourite music as much as possible.
Spend time on your own.
Wash your hands often, especially when in public.
Give back to the community.
Reduce, reuse, recycle, upcycle.
Educate but don't change people - let them be who they are.
Have integrity, be genuine and honest.
Don't get caught up on the small stuff.
Forgive but don't forget.

Move on with your head held high.
Clean your car regularly.
Help others without the need for gratification.
Consider others, the world doesn't revolve around you.
Remember, great wisdom is only achieved through great mistakes.

www.ingramcontent.com/pod-product-compliance
Lightning Source LLC
Chambersburg PA
CBHW062111140826
49812CB00058B/1265
*9789357212342*